MAKING ROBOT WARRIORS FROM JUNK

MAKING ROBOT WARRIORS FROM JUNK

BUILD 'EM WELL,
MAKE 'EM STRONG!
YOUR ENEMIES WILL BE SORRIER,
THEN WATCH 'EM BEAT
A SWIFT RETREAT
FROM YOUR ULTIMATE
ROBOT WARRIOR!

Greetings, Roboteers! Are you ready for some junk craft construction? First, let me introduce myself . . . Cyber Sid's the name. I'm a genuine RWAA-5500 (Robotic Warrior Assembly Autobot). In my time at the Robot Center, I've worked on dozens of battling vehicles, with serious weaponry and precision maneuvers. Each robot is built using household junk, so you'll be doing a great job as a recycler, something I am programmed to do every time I work on a new design,

There's a section on making each of the five Robot Warriors with step-by-step pictures and ideas for making them even more spectacular. I've also included a sheet of fantastic stickers to give your completed robots that extra advantage when they roll out into the Robodrome for battle. Choose the Robot Warrior you'd like to build first, and don't worry if the shapes of containers in the parts gallery are slightly different from the ones that you have. Your design will be just as good, if not better!

 PARTS GALLERY This section has photographs of all the junk and materials that you'll need to collect, plus hints and tips on where to find them.

 TOOL CHEST This has a list of recommended tools, as well as hints on how to use them safely.

 HAZARD WARNING These highlight important safety precautions and tasks that require adult supervision. Remember, a good Roboteer always puts safety first!

 TOP TIPS Get off to a flying start with the best tips from our top technicians at the Robot Center, and check out the hottest hints on construction techniques.

 ASSEMBLY BREAKDOWN This has instructions and pictures to show you how to put all those parts together.

 FINISHING There are ideas for paint effects and other fabulous finishing touches, including the best places to position your stickers to make your robot the coolest in the Robodrome.

ELECTRA EXTRA Think you're a technical wizard? Then take a look at the Electra Extra section. It has technical instructions and ideas for adding battery-powered motors, lights, and buzzers to your Robot Warriors. There are also instructions for building a superb remote control. You'll need the help of a friendly adult, but if you're a budding bright spark give it a shot!

CONTENTS

ADULT HELP RECOMMENDED

As you go through the manual, you will see this flash, which shows that certain items, tools, and skills need adult help, supervision, or advice. Remember, a first-class Roboteer never takes risks. Always work safely and follow the advice given in the hazard warnings in each section. As long as you do, you'll be unlikely to hurt yourself or others. Remember the safety rules: **Put safety first and you won't need first aid. Read all labels carefully. Ask adults for help. Use tools correctly. Never rush your work. Spot dangers before they spot you.**

PARTS GALLERY

Before you start, make sure you ask an adult for permission to help yourself to junk around the house. A shoe box or cardboard box is ideal for storing all your parts and tools in one place. Ask relatives and friends for junk — that way, you'll be encouraging them to recycle, too.

Baking powder or soda containers

Circular air fresheners, pulled apart, make great wheels

Wedge-shaped air freshener

Talcum powder containers

Large water bottles

Small water bottles with pop-up caps

Screw top lids come in all different sizes and colors

Pop-up caps from soft-drink bottles

Paper fasteners

Shower gel bottles with molded hooks

Shower gel bottles with flip hooks

⚠ HAZARDS

- CHECK THE HAZARD WARNING PANELS BEFORE STARTING ANY PROJECTS. IF YOU ARE UNSURE ABOUT ANYTHING, ASK AN ADULT.
- SOME CONTAINERS CONTAIN HARMFUL SUBSTANCES SUCH AS BLEACH. ALWAYS ASK AN ADULT IF IT IS SAFE TO USE THEM.
- ASK AN ADULT TO WASH USED CLEANING SUPPLY BOTTLES IN VERY HOT WATER!
- REFER TO THE TOP TIPS PANEL FOR IDEAS ON WHERE TO FIND OLD COMPUTER CIRCUIT BOARDS. REMEMBER, YOU SHOULD NEVER HANDLE ELECTRICAL EQUIPMENT THAT IS IN USE OR STILL PLUGGED IN.

Cardboard can be cut into shapes such as saw blades

Dressmaker's elastic cord

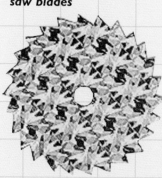

Shampoo bottles with flip-top lids

Wooden barbecue skewer

Wooden dowel

Electrical clips

TOP TIPS

● To modify robots for running on smooth, slippery surfaces, stretch small, wide rubber bands or a length of weatherproofing strip around the wheel rims for extra grip.

● Screw anchors are used for putting screws in walls. They look just the part as far as wheel spikes go.

● You should be able to find old circuit boards from any store that upgrades computers. They will probably have a whole box full of broken or out-of-date sound cards, video cards, and modems. You may have a circuit board at home already if someone in the house upgrades their own computer from time to time. But be sure to ask for permission before gluing someone's brand-new memory chips onto the back of Ramjet!

Bottles with spray nozzles

Old circuit boards

Drinking straws

CDs

Bulb and holder

Electrical speaker wire

35mm film containers

Cylindrical toilet roll holder

Buzzers

Pulley wheels

Battery connector

Battery holder

Rubber bands

A 1.5-volt DC electrical motor

Coat hangers can come in all different forms

Ping-Pong balls

A PILE OF JUNK... SOME ODDS AND ENDS,
YOU'VE GOT THE BASIC PARTS.
NOW GET TO WORK AND
MAKE THEM FIT.
THAT'S WHEN THE REAL
FUN STARTS!

screw anchors

Toothpicks

Coat hangers with pull-out ends

Electrical switches

TOOL CHEST

Although just a few simple tools are needed for these projects, you may find others that are very useful. Always ask an adult before you use a tool and make sure it is safe to use on your own.

You'll find you work better if you keep all your tools together in a clearly marked box. Make sure that saws, knives, and sharp tools are stored safely so you won't cut yourself when you get them out. Saws and knives are safer if they are kept clean and sharp — a blunt, dirty edge is more likely to slip.

SCISSORS (LARGE AND SMALL)
Scissors are very handy for all sorts of jobs, but always be careful with the sharp blades.

PLIERS
Great for twisting wires together in the Electra Extra section — a small pair of needle-nosed pliers is ideal.

AWL
A hot awl is best for making round holes. If you don't have one, use an old knitting needle.

JUNIOR HACKSAW
Fix the object in a vise or hold it firmly over the edge of a bench. Keep the saw upright and cut on the push-stoke (you don't need to push hard), using the whole length of the saw.

MARKER PEN
Choose one that will write on plastic.

CRAFT KNIVES
Craft knives must be sharp so that you don't need to press hard to cut. If you have to press hard, your hand is more likely to slip.

SOLDERING IRON
Great for fixing wires in place, but you MUST have adult help if you use them, because they get very hot.

SHARP BLADES AND SPIKES, AND HOT TOOLS, TOO — TREAT THEM RIGHT, RESPECT IS DUE. ALWAYS PUT YOUR SAFETY FIRST, AND WITH HAZARD WARNINGS BE WELL VERSED!

TEA-LIGHT CANDLES
Use these to heat an awl or craft knife to make holes or cuts in plastic.

ELECTRICAL TAPE

Available at all hardware stores. You'll need this to join wires together in the Electra Extra section!

DUST MASK

Available at most hardware stores. You MUST wear one of these if you are spray-painting your robots.

ACRYLIC PAINT

Many colors available from art supply stores. Ideal for spot painting plastic surfaces on robots. See Finishing, pages 10–11.

ARTISTS' PAINTBRUSHES

These can be bought at any art supply store and come in various sizes. Good for spot painting. See Finishing, pages 10–11.

MASKING TAPE

Ideal for masking off parts of your robots you don't want to paint! See Finishing, pages 10–11.

SPRAY PAINT

Great for applying large areas of color. ALWAYS wear a paint mask when using spray paint!

RUBBER GLOVES

Use for hot tool tasks, gluing, and spray-painting. You can buy them in supermarkets.

GLUE

The best option is a solvent-free contact adhesive. Always read the instructions on the packet. See the Hazards panel.

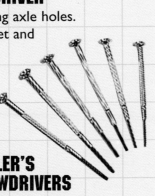

PHILLIPS SCREWDRIVER

For making axle holes. See Ramjet and Hatchet.

JEWELER'S SCREWDRIVERS

These delicate little screwdrivers may come in handy for the Electra Extra section.

⚠ HAZARDS

- ALWAYS FOLLOW SAFETY RULES AND WARNINGS — EVEN SIMPLE TOOLS CAN BE DANGEROUS IF YOU ARE NOT CAREFUL WHEN USING THEM. REMEMBER CYBER SID'S RHYME.
- ALWAYS STORE CRAFT KNIVES, SAWS, AND SCISSORS IN A SAFE PLACE WHEN NOT IN USE.
- MAKE SURE YOU WORK OUTSIDE OR IN A WELL–VENTILATED ROOM WHEN YOU ARE USING CONTACT ADHESIVE.
- IF YOU LIGHT A TEA-LIGHT CANDLE TO HEAT YOUR AWL, NEVER LEAVE IT UNATTENDED.
- STAND TOOLS, SUCH AS YOUR AWL, ON A HEAT-RESISTANT SURFACE AND KEEP A TUB OF COLD WATER NEARBY TO DIP IT INTO SO IT COOLS DOWN QUICKLY.
- IF YOU NEED TO CHANGE YOUR HACKSAW BLADE, ASK AN ADULT TO HELP YOU. REMEMBER TO SET THE NEW BLADE WITH ITS CUTTING TEETH POINTING FORWARD — SAWS CUT AS YOU PUSH FORWARD, NOT AS YOU PULL BACK.

HATCHET

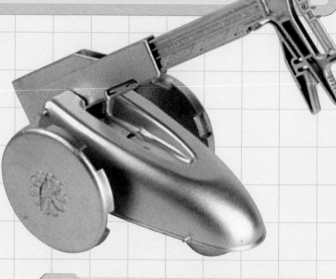

With its sleek, streamlined body, this Robot Warrior is quick and maneuverable. A smooth-running ball wheel at the front means that the Hatchet can compete in the most challenging races and obstacle courses. Add that to the powerful action of its hatchet arm and you have a winning combination.

PARTS

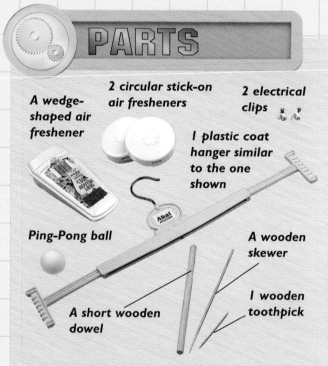

A wedge-shaped air freshener

2 circular stick-on air fresheners

2 electrical clips

1 plastic coat hanger similar to the one shown

Ping-Pong ball

A wooden skewer

A short wooden dowel

1 wooden toothpick

TOOLS

- A junior hacksaw
- Awl or an old knitting needle
- Craft knife
- Scissors
- A Phillips screwdriver that is slightly thicker than the wooden dowel
- A tea-light candle
- Glue

CHECK OUT THE ELECTRA EXTRA SECTION BEFORE YOU START IF YOU WOULD LIKE TO FIT A MOTOR TO HATCHET TO MAKE HIM WHIZZ ALONG!

ADULT HELP RECOMMENDED

YOU CAN BASH 'EM — YOU CAN CRASH 'EM — SO GET READY FOR SOME FUN. KEEP YOUR GRANNY SAFELY LOCKED INSIDE . . . WHEN HATCHET'S ON THE RUN.

HAZARD

- BE VERY CAREFUL WITH THE HOT AWL IN STEPS 2 AND 9, AND THE HOT CRAFT KNIFE IN STEP 8!

ASSEMBLY

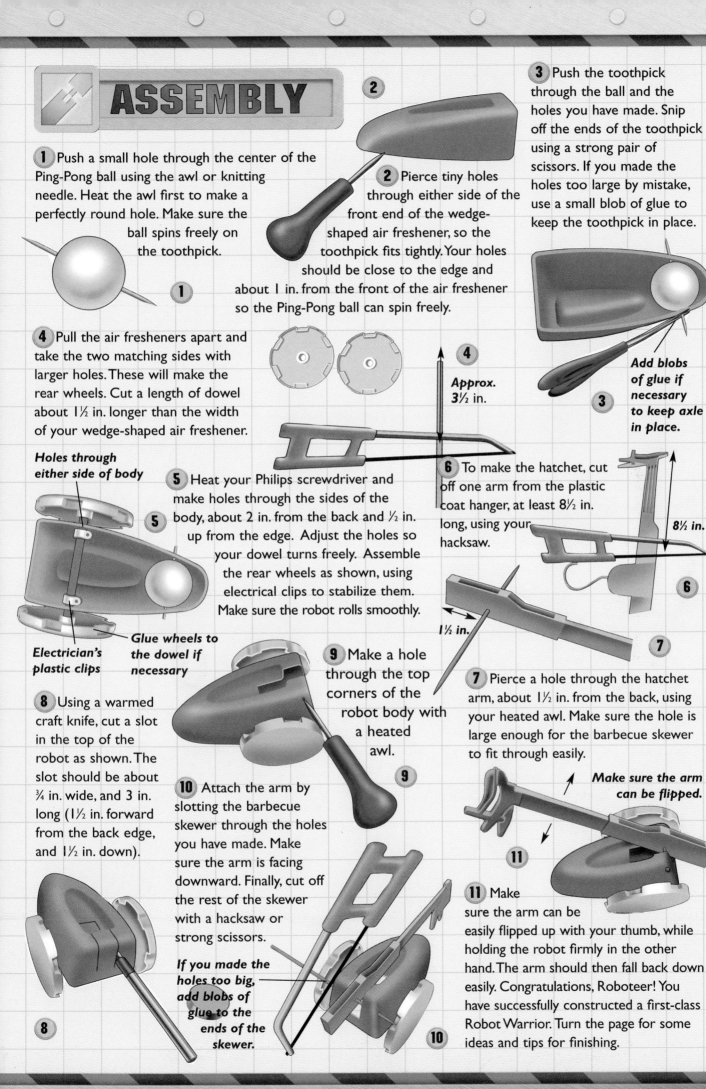

1 Push a small hole through the center of the Ping-Pong ball using the awl or knitting needle. Heat the awl first to make a perfectly round hole. Make sure the ball spins freely on the toothpick.

2 Pierce tiny holes through either side of the front end of the wedge-shaped air freshener, so the toothpick fits tightly. Your holes should be close to the edge and about 1 in. from the front of the air freshener so the Ping-Pong ball can spin freely.

3 Push the toothpick through the ball and the holes you have made. Snip off the ends of the toothpick using a strong pair of scissors. If you made the holes too large by mistake, use a small blob of glue to keep the toothpick in place.

Add blobs of glue if necessary to keep axle in place.

4 Pull the air fresheners apart and take the two matching sides with larger holes. These will make the rear wheels. Cut a length of dowel about 1½ in. longer than the width of your wedge-shaped air freshener.

Approx. 3½ in.

6 To make the hatchet, cut off one arm from the plastic coat hanger, at least 8½ in. long, using your hacksaw.

8½ in.

1½ in.

Holes through either side of body

5 Heat your Philips screwdriver and make holes through the sides of the body, about 2 in. from the back and ½ in. up from the edge. Adjust the holes so your dowel turns freely. Assemble the rear wheels as shown, using electrical clips to stabilize them. Make sure the robot rolls smoothly.

Electrician's plastic clips

Glue wheels to the dowel if necessary

9 Make a hole through the top corners of the robot body with a heated awl.

7 Pierce a hole through the hatchet arm, about 1½ in. from the back, using your heated awl. Make sure the hole is large enough for the barbecue skewer to fit through easily.

8 Using a warmed craft knife, cut a slot in the top of the robot as shown. The slot should be about ¾ in. wide, and 3 in. long (1½ in. forward from the back edge, and 1½ in. down).

10 Attach the arm by slotting the barbecue skewer through the holes you have made. Make sure the arm is facing downward. Finally, cut off the rest of the skewer with a hacksaw or strong scissors.

If you made the holes too big, add blobs of glue to the ends of the skewer.

Make sure the arm can be flipped.

11 Make sure the arm can be easily flipped up with your thumb, while holding the robot firmly in the other hand. The arm should then fall back down easily. Congratulations, Roboteer! You have successfully constructed a first-class Robot Warrior. Turn the page for some ideas and tips for finishing.

FINISHING

ADULT HELP RECOMMENDED

Car spray paints are ideal for adding sparkle to your robots. But be careful, because the paint comes out in a fine mist that will settle on anything within close range. Hang your robot on a clothesline with some thin string. (But not when there's laundry there!) Remove the lid and shake, shake, shake, to make the metal ball rattle! Count to at least 100 as you shake. Point the can away from you, with the nozzle about 8 in. away from your robot. Once the paint has set completely, decorate your robots with model paints, stickers or designs from your computer's paint program, and pictures from magazines.

TOOLS

- Rubber gloves
- Paint mask
- Masking tape
- Paintbrushes
- Cans of spray paint and jars of paint

⚠ HAZARD

- WHEN SPRAY-PAINTING, WEAR A PAINT MASK, OLD CLOTHES, AND RUBBER GLOVES.
- ALWAYS SPRAY AWAY FROM YOURSELF AND OTHER PEOPLE.

TOP TIPS

- You'll get a smoother finish if you use short, sharp bursts of spray paint.
- Keep moving around your robot so that you spray it from all directions.
- Let the paint dry before you go over it again, or blobs of runny paint will build up.
- If you do get blobs, let them dry, scrape them off with a craft knife, and spray the whole robot again.
- Let your robot dry for at least 3 hours. Handling it too soon will cause the paint to peel and rub away.

TAKE A PILE OF USELESS JUNK, CLEAN IT UP, WASH OUT THE GUNK. THEN WITH GLUE, SAW, AND CRAFT KNIFE BRING THAT PILE OF JUNK TO LIFE! SPINNING WHEELS, A CHOPPING ARM DESIGNED TO DEAL OUT UTMOST HARM. BEFORE YOU KNOW IT, YOU HAVE GOT A FIRST-CLASS WARRIOR ROBOT!

Here are some tips on painting techniques to help you decorate your robots before you add those funky stickers!

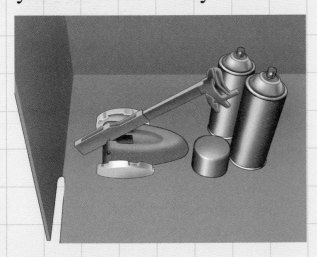

MAKING AND USING A SPRAY BOOTH

Hanging robots from the clothesline is fine on sunny, calm days. If the weather is bad or you have to work indoors, make a spray booth. A large cardboard box is ideal. Stand the box on its side with the flaps open. Put your robot near the back for spraying. Keep turning the robot to paint it all over.

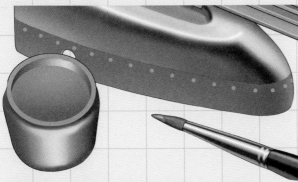

ADDING RIVETS AND BATTLE SCARS

Use a small brush to paint details such as rivets (above) and battle scars (below).

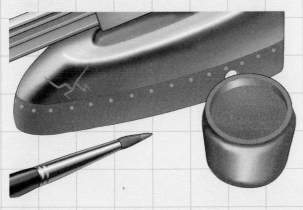

MASKING OFF

Use masking tape to create a two-tone effect. Press a strip of tape down firmly where you want a line. Smooth out kinks in the tape or the paint will "bleed" under it and spoil your nice crisp line. Make sure the paint is dry before you remove the tape or it will smudge.

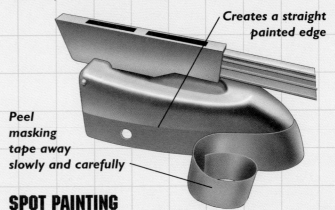

Creates a straight painted edge

Peel masking tape away slowly and carefully

SPOT PAINTING

Paint areas of your robot with a brush and contrasting colors to make them really stand out. Different parts of the body, wheels, and weapons can all be different colors. If you make a mistake, just wipe it off and start again.

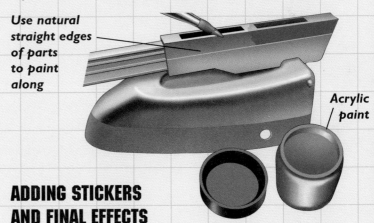

Use natural straight edges of parts to paint along

Acrylic paint

ADDING STICKERS AND FINAL EFFECTS

If all this talk about paint effects is bringing out the artist in you why not add exciting details to your robot, such as ferocious teeth, glaring red eyes, claws, camouflage stripes, or a lucky logo. A menacing look might even scare the opposition. Add the same kind of sticker on either side of your robot for a symmetrical, well-balanced look.

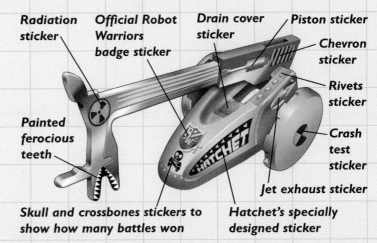

Radiation sticker

Official Robot Warriors badge sticker

Drain cover sticker

Piston sticker

Chevron sticker

Rivets sticker

Crash test sticker

Jet exhaust sticker

Painted ferocious teeth

Skull and crossbones stickers to show how many battles won

Hatchet's specially designed sticker

DOBERBOT

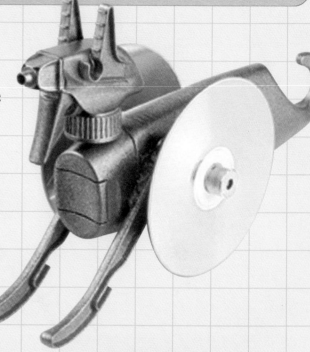

Two wheels are sometimes better than four, and Doberbot can roll, spin, rock, and perform a whole range of tricks on his two wheels. By controlling his tail, you can even get him to scoop up the enemy with a flick from those powerful front paws.

Always alert, Doberbot's head can turn in any direction. He is constantly on the lookout for intruders on his territory.

TOOLS

- A junior hacksaw
- Awl or old knitting needle
- Craft knife
- A tea-light candle
- Glue

CHECK OUT THE ELECTRA EXTRA SECTION BEFORE YOU START IF YOU LIKE THE IDEA OF MAKING DOBERBOT'S EYES GLOW RED WITH RAGE!

HAZARD

- BE CAREFUL WHEN USING A HOT KNITTING NEEDLE IN STEP 3. IT'S BEST TO USE A PAIR OF PLIERS TO HOLD THE HOT KNITTING NEEDLE.

PARTS

2 plastic coat hangers

2 water bottles with pop-up caps

Trigger action spray bottle

Wooden skewer

4 CDs

Shower gel dispenser with hook-shaped bottom

TEETH OF STEEL AND LASER EYES, THIS ROBOT'S GOT THE LOT. A BITE THAT'S MUCH WORSE THAN HIS BARK, OF COURSE... IT'S DOBERBOT!

ASSEMBLY

1 To make the body, unscrew the tops of your two water bottles and pry off the pop-up caps with a screwdriver or coin. Glue the two bottle tops to either side of the shower gel container as shown.

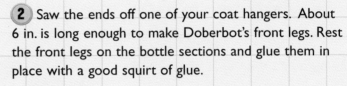

Saw the ends from coat hangers using a hacksaw. See tools section for tips on sawing with a hacksaw.

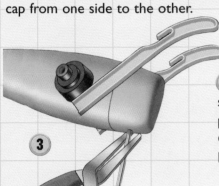

Keep the pop-up caps — you will need them later.

2 Saw the ends off one of your coat hangers. About 6 in. is long enough to make Doberbot's front legs. Rest the front legs on the bottle sections and glue them in place with a good squirt of glue.

5 Join Doberbot's head to its body through the holes you made earlier, cutting off the barbecue skewer with strong scissors or a hacksaw close to the body of the robot.

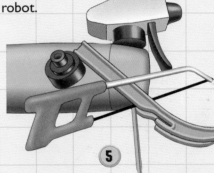

3 Heat a knitting needle in the tea-light candle flame. Hold it with a pair of pliers. Pierce a hole right through the shower gel cap from one side to the other.

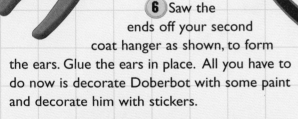

4 To make the head, unscrew the spray bottle top and pull off the plastic pipe that is attached to it. Glue your barbecue skewer into the hole where the pipe was attached.

Doberbot's ears should be standing up tall and alert, just like a real guard dog's.

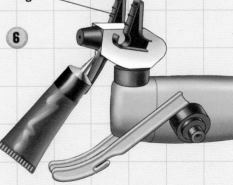

6 Saw the ends off your second coat hanger as shown, to form the ears. Glue the ears in place. All you have to do now is decorate Doberbot with some paint and decorate him with stickers.

FINISHING

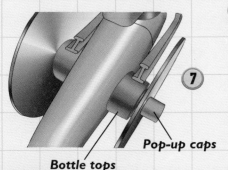

Pop-up caps

Bottle tops

7 When you have painted Doberbot, put on the wheels. Place two CDs together for each wheel — shiny sides outward. Press the bottle pop-up caps firmly into position. Another spot of glue may be needed to make sure your bottle tops are secure. Finally, decorate Doberbot with stickers.

Add Doberbot's specially designed sticker as shown.

CORPORAL BUZZ

With wide-tracked wheels, arching fenders and an angled, razor-sharp saw blade, Corporal Buzz is designed to cope with the roughest terrain and anything that dares to get in his way. An armor-plated ridge gives strength to his body shell, and rotating spikes on his wheels offer that extra element of surprise from the side.

PARTS

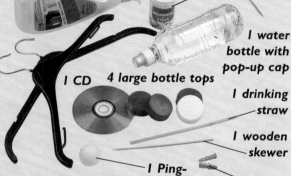

I trigger-action spray bottle

I baking powder container

I wooden toothpick

I water bottle with pop-up cap

I CD

4 large bottle tops

I drinking straw

I wooden skewer

2 plastic coat hangers

I Ping-Pong ball

2 screw anchors

CHECK OUT THE *ELECTRA EXTRA* SECTION TO FIND OUT HOW TO FIT A MOTOR. YOU'LL SOON HAVE THE CORPORAL BUZZING AROUND!

TOOLS

- A junior hacksaw
- Awl or old knitting needle
- Craft knife
- A tea-light candle
- Glue
- Strong scissors
- Marker pen

HAZARD

- BE CAREFUL WITH THE HOT AWL IN STEPS 1 AND 2, AND THE SCISSORS AND SHARP EDGES OF THE CD IN STEP 10!
- INSTEAD OF USING A CD, YOU COULD USE A CIRCLE OF CARDBOARD (ABOUT 5 IN. IN DIAMETER) TO MAKE YOUR SAW BLADE.

YOU'RE IN THE ARMY NOW. WATCH OUT FOR CORPORAL BUZZ! HE'LL CHEW YOU UP AND SPIT YOU OUT. THAT'S WHAT HIS BUZZ BLADE DOES.

ASSEMBLY

1 Make the main rear wheels by gluing the large bottle tops firmly together in pairs. Poke a hole through the center of both wheels using the awl.

(1)

A finished wheel

Large bottle tops

2 Using a heated awl, poke a hole through the spray bottle as shown. The holes should be about 2 in. from the bottom of the bottle. Make sure the skewer fits through the holes easily, without sticking at all.

2 in.

(2)

(3)

3 Assemble the rear wheels, using a small piece of plastic straw to keep the wheels away from the body. Leave enough skewer at either end to take the screw anchors. Glue the plugs and wheels in place, but make sure the whole axle spins freely.

4 Saw about 5 in. off each end of one of your coat hangers to form the fenders.

(4)

Coat hanger fender

5 Glue them in place above the rear wheels as shown.

Glue one coat hanger over the top edge of the robot as an armored spine.

Punched hole in wheel

(6)

6 Cut a 1/2 in. off the bottom of the baking powder container and push the top into it, to make a large, narrow wheel. Punch a hole through the center of the wheel, large enough to pass a toothpick through freely.

(5)

7 Cut a rectangular opening in the neck of the spray bottle large enough to take the front wheel. Punch a hole through the side of the neck, as close to the edge as possible, for the front axle.

Punched hole

(7)

Draw a tooth pattern along the edge of a CD with a marker pen.

8 Assemble the front wheel and axle, pushing the toothpick in place until it fits tightly through the holes in the bottle. The wheel should spin freely.

(8)

9 Remove the screw top from the drink bottle. Put the pop-up cap to one side. You'll need it later. Glue a Ping-Pong ball to the open end of the bottle. Glue the screw top of the water bottle to the Ping-Pong ball, at a 45-degree angle.

(9)

FINISHING

(10)

10 Warm the CD in hot water to soften it. With strong scissors, cut out the triangular pieces to make the teeth. Keep dipping the CD in hot water to keep it soft. Put the saw blade somewhere safe, to be attached later.

Once the paint is dry, fit the saw blade onto its housing and secure it with the pop-up cap that you kept earlier. So how does it feel to have created such a mechanical marvel? You are well on the way to becoming an experienced robot builder. If you have two Robot Warriors, turn to the Battle Bank to try some tactics and maneuvers. Or keep on bot-building!

Add Corporal Buzz's specially designed sticker as shown.

Pop-up cap

ROBODOZER

It's a robot. It's a bulldozer. It's Robodozer! Not only does this robot have the strength of its toothed shovel out front to scoop up the opposition, but on top it has a catapulting cage, capable of firing marbles and other small objects right into the heart of the enemies' defenses. Wicked wheel spikes will dent and damage other robot body shells as they pass by.

PARTS

A ribbed water bottle

A flip-top shower-gel bottle with fold-away hinge

1 cylindrical toilet roll holder

2 circular air fresheners

A length of dressmaker's elastic cord

2 plastic screw anchors

A bendy plastic straw

2 wooden skewers

TOOLS

- A junior hacksaw
- Awl or old knitting needle
- Craft knife
- Strong scissors
- A tea-light candle
- Glue

HAZARD

- BE CAREFUL WHEN USING THE HOT AWL IN STEPS 1, 2, AND 8. ALSO BEWARE OF SHARP SCISSORS IN STEPS 4 AND 10!

YOU'D BETTER ALL SHOUT — YOU'D BETTER ALL CRY, YOU'D BETTER WATCH OUT — I'M TELLING YOU WHY— ROBO-DOZER'S COMING TO TOWN! ROBO-DOZER'S COMING TO TOWN! RO — BO — DO — ZER'S COMING TO TOWN!

CHECK OUT THE ELECTRA EXTRA SECTION BEFORE YOU START IF YOU WOULD LIKE TO FIT A MOTOR TO ROBO TO MAKE HIM WHIZZ ALONG!

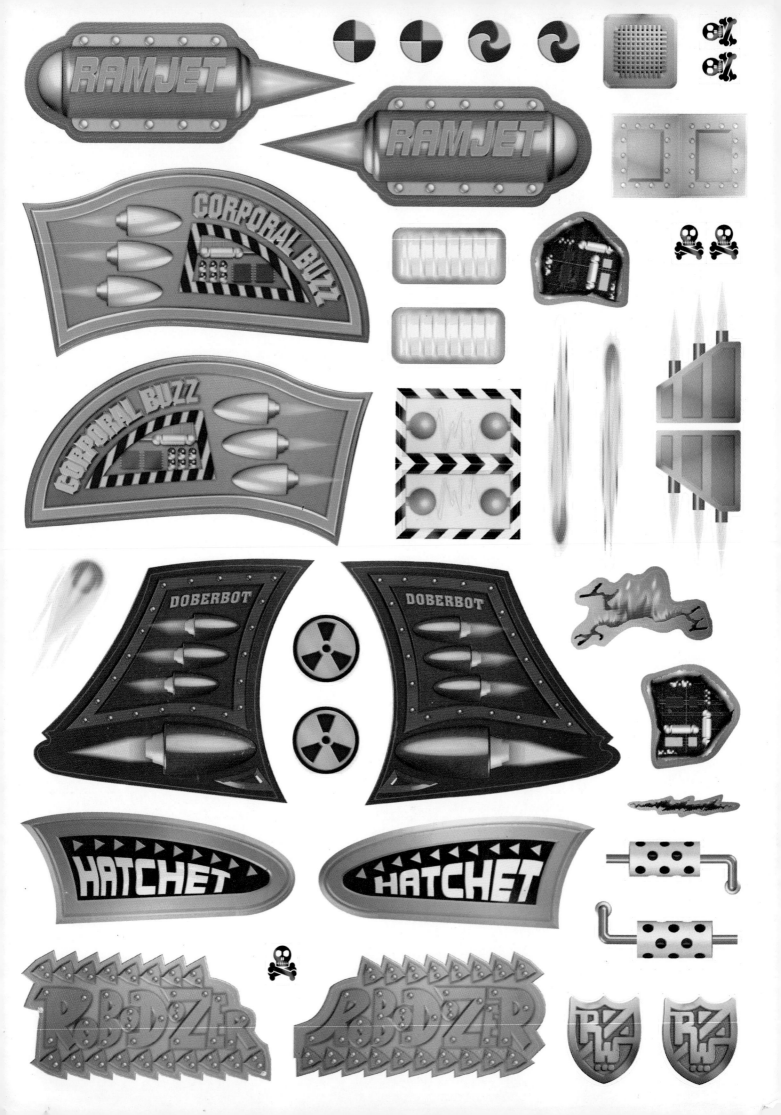

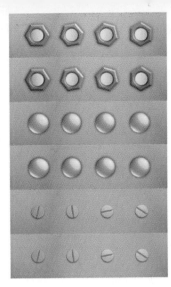

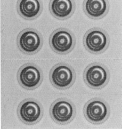

ASSEMBLY

1 Make a hole in each side of your bottle, about 1½ in. from the back, using a heated awl or knitting needle. A skewer should fit easily through the holes so that the rear wheels spin freely.

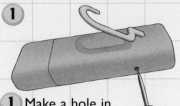

End taken off holder

4 Cut the hook off the toilet roll holder with scissors, then take off the end so that one side is open.

7 Punch a hole in the catapult arm about halfway up with a heated awl. Thread the end of the elastic through the hole. Pull the elastic (not too tight) and tie about two or three knots to secure it.

Hole pierced in catapult arm

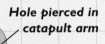

10 Cut a section from the ribbed water bottle with your scissors. This should be about seven ribbed sections long and 2 in. wide. Snip small triangles from the wider edge. This is Robo's shovel.

2 Separate the two air fresheners and remove the scented disks. Choose the two identical halves with the smaller holes at their center. Using your awl, punch holes through the center.

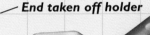

5 Glue the holder into the shampoo bottle hook with the open end facing forward.

8 Pierce a hole through the body of the robot with your awl next to the spot where the catapult arm is hinged. The hole should go right through the bottle.

11 Glue the shovel to the flip-up flap at the front of your robot. Use a generous blob of glue to hold the plastic shovel in place.

3 Slot the rear wheels onto the axle as shown, fitting a small section of straw (about 2 in.) between the robot body and wheel. Leave just enough skewer extending out of the wheel ends so that you can glue a screw anchor to each end. Make sure the wheels spin smoothly and evenly.

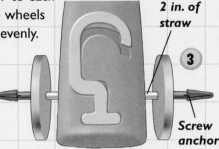

2 in. of straw

Screw anchor

6 Remove the lid of the bottle and punch a hole through the side opposite the hinge with your awl. Thread one end of the elastic through the hole and tie at least two knots on the end. Put the lid back on so that the elastic is on the top of the robot.

9 Glue a piece of skewer through both holes so that about ¾ in. sticks up in front of the catapult arm. This will stop the arm from firing too far forward and missing its target.

FINISHING

Give Robodozer a sparkling finish. If the shovel keeps falling off, you can make a stronger joint. Make two holes with a heated awl through the shovel and bottle flap. Now glue two short screws or pieces of matchstick into the holes, pushing them right through the shovel and into the flap. That should do it! Now grab some marbles and turn to the Battle Bank for some target practice.

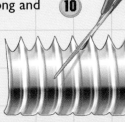

Add Robodozer's specially designed sticker as shown.

RAMJET

Built for power and speed, Ramjet can launch himself directly at the approaching contender with all the fury of a charging bull. Its body-piercing ram is designed to penetrate even the toughest armor and inflict maximum damage to the opponent's internal circuitry. Extra features include a rubber-powered drive shaft and real electronic components.

PARTS

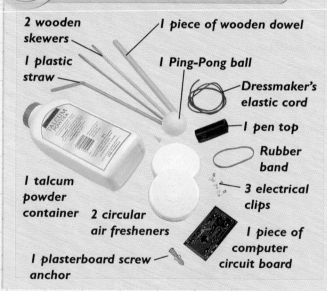

- 2 wooden skewers
- 1 piece of wooden dowel
- 1 plastic straw
- 1 Ping-Pong ball
- Dressmaker's elastic cord
- 1 pen top
- Rubber band
- 3 electrical clips
- 1 talcum powder container
- 2 circular air fresheners
- 1 piece of computer circuit board
- 1 plasterboard screw anchor

CHECK OUT THE ELECTRA EXTRA INSTRUCTIONS ON HOW TO GIVE RAMJET MOTORISED BATTERING POWER!

TOOLS

- A junior hacksaw
- Awl or old knitting needle
- Craft knife
- A tea-light candle
- Glue
- Phillips screwdriver — slightly wider than the dowel

HAZARD

- YOU SHOULD NEVER BE IN SUCH A HURRY THAT SAFETY COMES SECOND. REMEMBER THE CORRECT ORDER . . . SAFETY FIRST!

WHEELS THAT SQUEAL AND RAM OF STEEL, THE ENEMY SHOULD WORRY. THEY CAN'T ESCAPE THEIR AWFUL FATE, FROM RAMJET'S MIGHTY FURY!

1 Cut a rectangular hole in one side of the talcum powder container to gain access to the inside. Make holes in either side of the robot body large enough for the dowel to fit through easily.

Large rectangular hole

Heated screwdriver

1

2 Separate two air fresheners and use the two halves with the larger holes at their center. Use the discarded ones to make Robodozer. Cut a length of dowel about 1½ in. wider than the body.

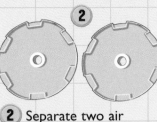

2

3 Slot in the axle and glue the rear wheels to it. Make sure the wheels spin freely. Remove the nails and push electrical clips between the wheels and body. Glue one clip, with its nail in place, to the center of the axle.

Electrical clips hold wheels in place

3

Electrical clip fixed to axle

4

4 Make a hole in the top of the robot body near the front. Thread your elastic through the hole and tie at least two knots in the end.

5 Thread enough elastic to reach just past the rear axle, tie a loop in the end, and hook it over the electrical clip nail.

5

6 Make a hole in the Ping-Pong ball with a heated awl so that a skewer fits through easily and the ball spins freely. Push holes into the side of the robot at least 1½ in. back from the front edge. Assemble the front wheel using pieces of plastic straw as spacers.

1½ in.

Holes through ball (front wheel) to hold axle

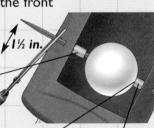

Straw spacers stop the Ping-Pong ball from moving sideways

Holes for axle

6

Pen top

7

8

7 Using a heated awl, punch a hole through the back of the robot close to the top edge and one in the center of the cap.

9

9 Make a slot across the end of the pen top with the heated awl.

8 Insert a skewer all the way until it comes out of the front and glue a screw anchor onto the skewer. Glue a pen top to the rear of the skewer.

Screw anchor

9

Glue the circuit board in place on top of your robot, spray the whole thing, and you're in business. To power up Ramjet's elastic motor, hook the elastic over the nail on the back axle. Holding the robot firmly in one hand, wind the rear wheels backward until the elastic is tight. Now place it on a carpeted or rough surface and let go . . .

Add Ramjet's specially designed sticker as shown.

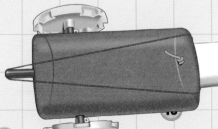

10 Stretch a rubber band over the neck of the bottle and hook it over the slot you made in the pen top. Pull the pen top back, then let go, and the ram will operate.

BATTLE BANK

Building a robot is one thing, but learning to operate it is another. So check out the Top Tips panel first and try out your robot operating skills.

Once you have mastered these skills, mark out a Robodrome arena for your battles. Use an indoor floor space or an outdoor patio to compete on. Collect objects, such as the ones shown here, to build obstacles and challenges for each robot. The more robots you have the more fun your battles will be, so encourage your friends to build their own robots and pit their champions against yours for real head-to-head competitions. Make your own scoreboard or use the score sheet on page 23.

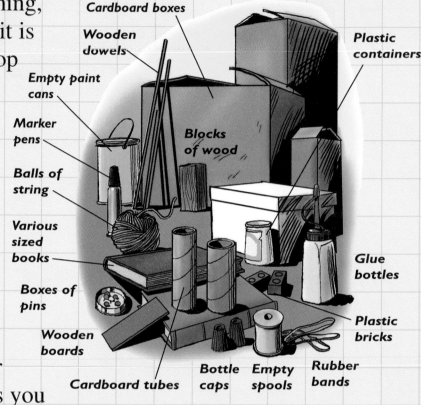

Cardboard boxes
Wooden dowels
Plastic containers
Empty paint cans
Marker pens
Blocks of wood
Balls of string
Various sized books
Glue bottles
Boxes of pins
Plastic bricks
Wooden boards
Cardboard tubes
Bottle caps
Empty spools
Rubber bands

TOP TIPS

● Make sure your robot's wheels are accurately lined up and well-balanced. This will make all the difference in the heat of the battle.

● Practice flipping Hatchet's arm with your thumb.

● Improve your wrist action when spinning Corporal Buzz's saw blade.

● Try out a range of scoops and flips with Doberbot and Robodozer.

● Even a simple mechanism, such as Ramjet's elastic powered ram, can be very effective if used at just the right moment. Timing is crucial.

IN BATTLE BANK YOU'LL FIND A STORE OF CHALLENGES AND TASKS GALORE. PICK THE BEST — INVENT YOUR OWN — THE CHOICE IS YOURS IN THE ROBODROME.

THE ALPHA CHALLENGE

Lay out a long, straight line of string or yarn on the ground. You can tape the ends in place to stop it from moving. Now see how accurately you can propel your robot along this line without it veering off. To score points your robot should travel not less than 1 yard along the line and stay as close as possible to the string. Score 30 points for a perfect finish. Take away 5 points for every ½ inch that you stray off course.

THE BETA CHALLENGE

Build a pyramid of spools, each row having one less than the last, until you have one spool on top. From a distance of 5 feet, launch your robot at the wall. Score 5 points for every spool knocked down and an extra 10 points if you knock the whole wall down in one go.

Glue two pieces of dowel into plywood at back

A piece of elastic tied to the dowels makes a catapult

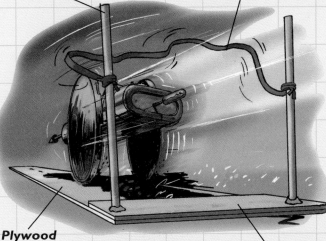

Plywood runway

Piece of plywood glued to back of runway

THE GAMMA CHALLENGE

Set up a long-distance trial. Mark out a starting line, then see which robot can travel the farthest with one push. Score 50 points for the winning long-distance run. Experiment with different ways of launching your robots:
• Push by hand.
• Make a ramp using a piece of thin plywood to start your robots off.
• Use elastic to motorize all your robot's rear wheels as shown in Ramjet's assembly breakdown.
• Make an elastic robot launcher as shown in the picture.

THE DELTA CHALLENGE

Set up a jump course using two ramps. The idea is to see how far your robots can travel. Increase the gap between your ramps until none of your robots can make the distance. Score an increasing number of points for each gap your robot leaps.
4 in. = 5 points
8 in. = 10 points
12 in. = 20 points
16 in. = 40 points
20 in. = 80 points   And so on . . .
Launch your robots by hand or make an elastic launcher as shown in the picture above.

THE EPSILON CHALLENGE

If your robot has a missile launcher, such as the one on Robodozer, set up some targets to aim for. Targets could either be a row of small objects to knock down, or a paper scoring target with points getting higher and a bull's-eye at the center worth 50 points.

THE ZETA CHALLENGE

To test the speed of your robots, tie a thin string to the front of each one. For this challenge, you will need a different person throwing a dice. The dice thrower rolls a dice over and over again until a six is rolled. Once a six has been thrown, the robot must quickly escape by being pulled out of reach before being captured by the dice thrower. The robot is captured by bringing the hand straight down onto the string, preventing its escape. Score 10 points for each successful escape, with a maximum of five attempts.

THE ETA CHALLENGE

Attach objects such as marbles to the tops of two robots using small blobs of Fun-Tak or double-sided tape. Bash and crash your robots against each other until one of them loses its marbles! The winner gets 80 points. Robots can use any of their weapons, scoops, and special features to help them win in this challenge.

THE THETA CHALLENGE

Set up a goal-scoring challenge. Place two empty spools on the ground as goalposts. Use a Ping-Pong ball and try to score goals by firing your robot at the ball. Score 30 points for each goal scored. You can make this more challenging by adding a robot goalie. There is a score sheet for you to photocopy on the opposite page, to keep a record of your scores.

SCORE SHEET

ALPHA

BETA

GAMMA

DELTA

EPSILON

ZETA

ETA

THETA

ELECTRA EXTRA

So you think you're a budding electrical wizard? Rubber bands aren't good enough, hmm? Then you're the kind of roboteer we're looking for at the Robot Center. With the right components you can achieve electrifying results! Specialized tools aren't essential, but a pair of wire strippers will come in handy. A soldering iron is the best tool for joining wires, but it can get very hot, so you must have adult help. Wires can also be twisted and held in place with electrical tape. Explore your local hobby shop and look at adding motors, colored lights, and noisy buzzers to any of the robots.

TOOLS

- **Wire strippers**
- **Soldering iron**
- **Electrical tape**

HAZARD

- ASK AN ADULT TO HELP YOU IF YOU PLAN TO USE A SOLDERING IRON IN THIS SECTION.

PARTS

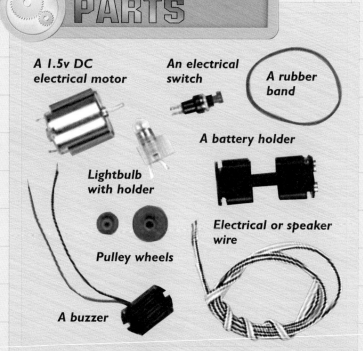

A 1.5v DC electrical motor

An electrical switch

A rubber band

A battery holder

Lightbulb with holder

Pulley wheels

Electrical or speaker wire

A buzzer

HERE'S A REALLY SUPER TIP, TO GIVE YOUR ROBOTS EXTRA ZIP. ADD MOTORS, LIGHTS AND BUZZERS, TOO, WITH ELECTRA EXTRA, IT'S UP TO YOU!

ATTACHING LIGHTS AND BUZZERS

1 Make a hole in the back of Hatchet's shell with a heated awl and fit the switch, securing it with the nut provided.

2 Make a small hole in the front for the two buzzer wires to pass through, and glue the buzzer in place.

3 Solder two wires onto the switch terminals. Connect one of these to a buzzer wire and the other to one end of the battery.

4 Connect the other end of the battery to the other buzzer wire (shown in black in the picture in step 3). Space is limited, so you can do away with a battery holder by soldering wires to the battery. When your battery runs down, just solder another one in to replace it.

5 Try putting on a lightbulb to dazzle the opposition. Remember, lights and buzzers are great, but the more you have, the more power you use, so your batteries won't last as long. If you use Light Emitting Diodes (LEDs, which usually come in red and green), they must be wired up with current flowing in the right direction.

FITTING A MOTOR TO CORPORAL BUZZ

1 Push the small pulley wheel firmly onto the motor spindle.

4 Fit the wheels in place and stretch a rubber band over the two pulley wheels. Putting a twist in the rubber band to form a figure eight will stop it from slipping off too easily.

2 Slot the motor into the holder and glue the unit onto the back of Corporal Buzz. Using a holder allows you to adjust the position of the motor once it is in place.

5 Glue the battery holder in place on the back of Corporal Buzz. Make sure there is enough room to remove the batteries when they run out.

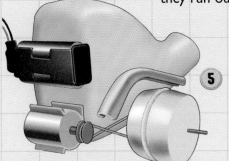

3 Glue the other pulley wheel onto the rear wheel and axle.

6 Connect one strand of the speaker wire to the motor and the other strand to the battery terminal wire. The other battery terminal wire should also be connected directly to the motor.

7 Connect the other end of the speaker wire to your switch. Solder the wires into place after twisting them onto the terminals

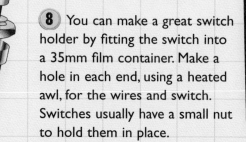

8 You can make a great switch holder by fitting the switch into a 35mm film container. Make a hole in each end, using a heated awl, for the wires and switch. Switches usually have a small nut to hold them in place.

9 That's it! Now you have a simple remote control unit to send your robot into battle, 3-2-1 . . . charge! If you handled that easily and would like to make a more complex remote control unit with forward and reverse capabilities, then stand by for my Do-it-yourself Remote Control.

FITTING MOTORS TO OTHER ROBOTS

RAMJET

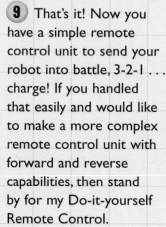

BASIC WIRING CIRCUIT FOR FITTING MOTORS

With the other three robots, the basic method of wiring up the motor is shown here. Attach one wire from the battery holder to the motor, twisting it together securely. Attach wires from the motor to the switch and from the switch back to the battery holder to form a circuit. A soldering iron will make much better joints, but ask an adult to help you.

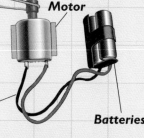

Pulley wheel   Rubber band   **Motor**

Wires

Batteries

HATCHET

For Hatchet and Ramjet, glue the motor inside the body shell as shown in the diagrams. Robodozer and Corporal Buzz work best if you attach the motor to the outside of the body shell at the back. The axle pulley wheel is also on the outside for both of these robots.

TOP TIPS

- Unfortunately, Doberbot cannot be motorized easily. If you want him to have a motor, you will need to redesign his wheels so that they have an axle. But hey! How about wiring up LEDs to give Doberbot some super glow-in-the-dark red eyes! (See: Attaching Lights and Buzzers, on page 25.)
- If possible, glue the battery holder inside your robot so it is out of the way. Glue motors so that the motor pulley wheel lines up with the pulley wheel on the axle (see diagrams above).
- Make sure you use the right size rubber band — it should be tight, but not so tight that the wheels don't turn.
- If your robot moves back instead of forward, don't panic. Remove the rubber band, twist it to make a figure eight and put it back on. Your robot will now move forward. This is easier than undoing the wires and changing the direction of the current.

Motor fits on back   **ROBODOZER**

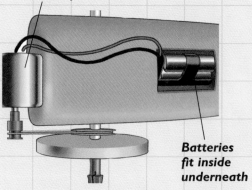

Batteries fit inside underneath

On Hatchet and Ramjet, put a rubber band over the pulley before you attach the axle. Leave one wheel unglued so you can replace broken bands easily. Corporal Buzz and Robodozer can have rubber bands fitted later.

DIY REMOTE CONTROL SWITCH

If you're feeling really adventurous, how about building your own two-way switch in a hand-held controller. This controller can also hold the batteries to power your robot, so there's no need to fit them to the body shell. Here's how to do it.

Electrical do-it-yourself remote control

Ping-Pong ball control knob

PARTS

A flat bottle, such as a shower gel bottle

Electrical speaker wire

A rubber band

A Ping-Pong ball

A skirt hanger

8 brass paper fasteners

A wooden skewer

TOOLS

- Awl or old knitting needle
- Glue
- Strong scissors
- Craft knife
- Junior hacksaw
- Marker pen

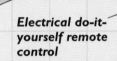

TO START 'EM UP REALLY QUICK, A SIMPLE SWITCH MIGHT DO THE TRICK. REMOTE CONTROL IS MUCH MORE FUN, SO WHY NOT CHECK OUT HOW IT'S DONE?

HAZARD

- SOME STEPS IN THE DO-IT-YOURSELF REMOTE CONTROL SECTION ARE COMPLICATED AND CAN BE HAZARDOUS, SO ASK AN ADULT TO HELP YOU.
- THE SAFETY WARNINGS GIVEN SO FAR FOR ALL THE PROJECTS IN THIS MANUAL APPLY TO THE USE OF TOOLS HERE. PLEASE CHECK THEM AGAIN AND PUT SAFETY FIRST.

1 Cut a slot 2 in. long and ½ in. wide in each flat side of the shower gel bottle. Then punch holes in the sides of the bottle, as shown, using a heated awl. The holes should line up exactly with the centers of the slots.

2 in.

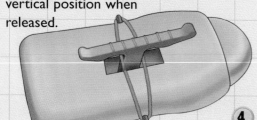

Punch holes on both sides of the bottle

2 Remove one arm from the skirt hanger and saw off the end to make a control stick at least 4½ in. long. Punch a hole half-way along using a heated awl.

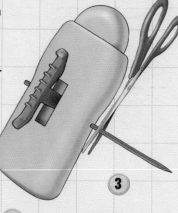

2

4½ in.

3

3 Push a barbecue skewer through the side holes of the bottle and control stick. Snip off the ends of the skewer so that about a ¼ in. sticks out of each side.

4 Hook a rubber band over the two skewer ends across the bottle. The band should go around on either side of the control arm so that it springs back to a vertical position when released.

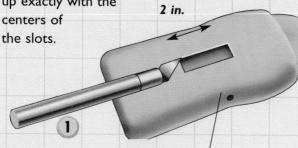

4

5 Cut a slot in the Ping-Pong ball with a warmed craft knife. Glue the ball to the sawed off end of the control arm. (See picture on page 27.)

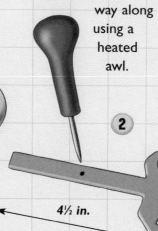

5

6

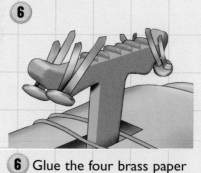

6 Glue the four brass paper fasteners onto the control arm head, pointing diagonally downward as shown.

7 Rock the arm forward and with a marker mark the points where each of the four fasteners touches the surface of the bottle.

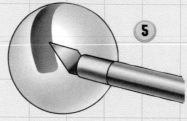

7

8 Punch holes with the awl where you made marks with the marker. The holes should be large enough to push paper fasteners through easily.

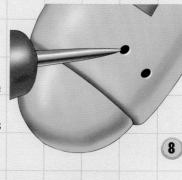

8

9 Strip the plastic from the ends of four lengths of wire. Two should be about 8 in. long and the other two 4½ in. Attach each wire to a paper fastener. Push the wires through the holes and out through the open neck of the bottle. The two shorter wires should be fed through the holes nearest to the neck.

Wire with end stripped away

9

10 To remember which wire is which, put a black dot on one paper faster head and a black line around the other end of the wire. The next fastener would have two dots on its head and two bands on the end of the wire and so on.

10

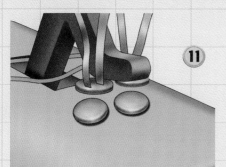

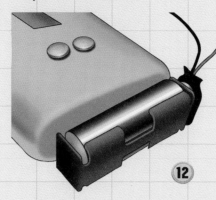

12 Glue a battery holder to the bottom of the bottle. It is easier to replace batteries if this stays on the outside.

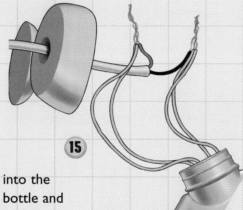

12

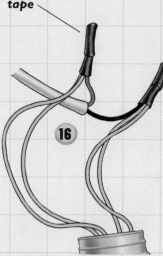

Electrical tape

16

11 Press the fasteners into their holes and secure each one with a blob of glue. Be careful not to get glue on the tops of the brass heads themselves.

13 Attach the two battery wires to the nearest two heads on the control arm. Solder or a blob of glue will hold them in place.

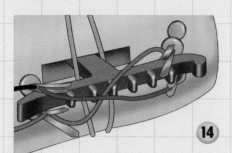

14

15 Take a long controller wire (speaker wire is best) and thread it through the bottle top. Twist the long and short wires on each side of the controller arm together to make a pair of leads. Twist a wire from the long controller lead to each of the pairs of leads.

14 Fasten two short wires across the control arm head as shown. Make sure you cross them over to reverse the polarity of the battery to the other wires to give you reverse gear. Solder or tape the wires to the brass fasteners, making sure there is a good contact.

15

16 Stick a piece of electrical tape over the twisted wires so the bare ends are totally covered.

17 Push the wires into the neck of the bottle and replace the lid.

17

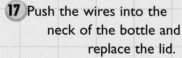

FINISHING

18 Connect the two long controller wires to the robot motor and secure them in place with solder. You could use alligator clips if you don't want the wires to be connected permanently.

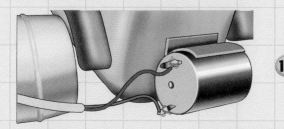

18

Make sure your connections are secure, you have charged batteries, and a rubber band runs from the motor to the axle pulley wheel. Your remote should now bring your robot buzzing to life! If the rubber band slips from the motor or wheel, make a figure-eight loop in it. That should stop it from slipping, but it will reverse the direction of the wheels. Spray your remote control, but make sure you don't spray electrical connectors such as the paper fasteners. Cover them with masking tape, and when the paint is dry, add the arrow stickers to the control stick (see picture on page 27).

Do-it-yourself remote control arrow sticker

ADULT HELP RECOMMENDED

NEW GENERATION

If you've had fun making the robots so far, don't stop here. You have learned new skills and techniques, so why not use them to design and build your own robots?

Don't forget, for a first-class Roboteer anything is possible — and it all starts with an idea. Remember to use your tools carefully and put safety first at all times.

I hope you have enjoyed your training and studies so far. Keep practicing those maneuvers in the Robodrome, and farewell for now, Roboteers!

WEBSITES

The Internet is an exciting place to search for information on robots. There are books for sale on robot construction, videos, photos, and much more. Here are a few of my favorite websites:

www.robotbooks.com
A great collection of books and links on robot Fhobbies and clubs. Click on "Robolinks," too.

www.robotics.nasa.gov
Nasa's official site for all that's robotic.

www.robosaurus.com
Check out the world's only 40-foot car-munching monsterbot — great photos, info, and videos!

www.robotcombat.com
Links to battling robot competitions and TV shows.

www.battlebots.com
The official US Web site of Comedy Central's Battlebots

www.robotwars.co.uk
The official UK Web site of the BBC's Robotwars.

www.robotbuilders.net
Serious robot construction based on famous film robots.

DESIGN TOP TIPS

● Look around the house for strange and unusual plastic bottles and containers. Weird shapes will fire your imagination when you start designing.

● Be creative with different shapes and sizes of circular plastic tops and containers to make your robot's wheels.

● Keep an eye out for small plastic odds and ends, such as pen tops and broken toy parts. You can use these in your design to make your robot stands out from the rest in the Robodrome.

● Experiment with paint effects and other finishing touches. Use oil- or acrylic-based model paints as well as spray paints to decorate your robots. Personalize your robot by designing your own stickers.

IF YOU'VE REACHED THE END AND MADE THE GRADE, GREAT! CONGRATULATIONS! YOU'RE READY NOW TO TRY YOUR HAND AT AN "ALL-NEW GENERATION."

I WISH YOU WELL, YOUNG ROBOTEERS, AND LAST FAREWELLS I BID. SO, BON VOYAGE AND CHEERIO! YOURS TRULY, CYBER SID!

GLOSSARY

Acrylic paint — resin-based paint that can be diluted with water.

Alligator clips — small metal clips with teeth that can be used to join wires together.

Alpha (beta, gamma, delta, epsilon, zeta, eta, theta) — letters of the Greek alphabet.

CD — Compact disk.

Circuit board — a thin board containing electrical components (parts) and circuits.

Diameter — the distance from one edge of a circle to the other, across the center.

Electrical circuit — components that work when electricity flows through them, usually from one pole of a battery to the other.

Electrical clips — small, plastic clips with a small nail in them, used to attach wires and cables to walls.

Electrical motor (1.5v DC) — a small machine that runs on battery power. The "**v**" stands for volts, and shows the strength of electrical current. **DC** stands for Direct Current, where the electricity flows in one direction from one pole of the battery to the other pole.

Electrical tape — Also called insulating tape. Sticky, stretchy tape used for wrapping around bare wires to stop them from touching other wires and interfering with your circuit. As a safer alternative to soldering, you can twist wires together firmly and cover the ends with small pieces of the tape.

LEDs — Light Emitting Diodes. Small electrical components that glow, usually green or red. These will only glow when the electricity is flowing in the right direction. You will have to experiment to find out which way works and which doesn't.

Maneuvers — a series of movements requiring skill and care.

Mechanism — a set of moving parts that work together.

Motorize — to add a motor.

Phillips screwdriver — a screwdriver with a narrow star-shaped end, rather than a wide, flat end.

Robodrome — a specially designed arena or stadium for battling robots and challenges of skill.

Screw anchors — small plastic parts for holding screws in walls.

Soldering — joining wires or metal surfaces using a soldering iron. The soldering iron is used to melt and apply the solder (a mixture of two or more metals) to the surfaces that need to be joined.

Tea-light candle — a small safety candle in a metal holder.

Wooden skewer — a long, thin piece of wood for holding food together in cooking.

ISBN 0-439-33891-3

Text © 2002 by Stephen Munzer.

All rights reserved. Published by Scholastic Inc., 557 Broadway, New York, NY 10012. The Chicken House is published in the United States in association with Scholastic.

SCHOLASTIC and associated logos are trademarks and/or registered trademarks of Scholastic Inc. THE CHICKEN HOUSE and associated logos are trademarks of The Chicken House.

12 11 10 9 8 7 6 5 4 3 2 1   2 3 4 5 6 7/0

Printed in the U.S.A.

First Scholastic printing, July 2002

Illustrators: Push Creative, Roger Goode, Roger Wade-Walker
Photography by Simon Powell